Graphic layout, designer & art consultant
Fabio Riccobono

COLD SMOKING & MEAT GAME

THE ULTIMATE GUIDE TO SMOKE MEAT, FISH, AND GAME.
HOW TO MAKE EVERYTHING FROM DELICIOUS MEALS TO TASTY TREATS.

LIAM WILLIAMS

TABLE
OF CONTENTS

INTRODUCTION

WHAT IS A PELLET SMOKER AND GRILL?

To provide you with a clear answer about the Wood Pellet Smoker and Grill, let us start by defining this grilling appliance. In fact, Pellet Smoker and Grills can be defined as an electric outdoor Smoker and Grill that is only fueled by wood pellets. Wood Pellet is a type of fuel that is characterized by its capsule size and is praised for its ability to enhance more flavors and tastes to the chosen smoked meat. And what is unique and special about wood pellet as a fuel is that it can grill, smoke, roast, braise and even bake according to its easy to follow instructions. I equipped with a control board that allows you to automatically maintain your desired temperature for several hours

WHY CHOOSE TO USE A WOOD PELLET SMOKER AND GRILL?

Accurate, Pellet Smoker and Grills make an explosive mixture of sublime tastes and incredible deliciousness; it is a great Smoker and Grill appliance that you can use if you want to enjoy the taste of charcoal grill and at the same time you don't want to give up on the traditional taste of ovens. And what is more interesting about pellet Smoker and Grills is that, with a single button, you can grill, roast, bake, braise and smoke, your favorite meat portions.

HOW TO USE A WOOD PELLET SMOKER AND GRILL?

Pellet Smoker and Grills function based on advanced digital technology and many mechanical parts. The pellet Smoker and Grill are then lit while the temperature is usually programmed with the help of a digital control board. Pellet Smoker and Grills work by using an algorithm so that it allows calculating the exact number of pellets you should use to reach the perfect temperature. Every Wood Pellet Grill is equipped with a rotating auger that allows to automatically feed the fire right from the hopper to the fire to maintain the same temperature. And even as the food continues cooking, the wood pellet Smoker and Grill will continue to drop the exact number of pellets needed to keep the perfect cooking temperature. But what can we cook with a pellet Smoker and Grill?

WHAT DISHES CAN WE PREPARE ON A WOOD PELLET SMOKER AND GRILL?

Thanks to its versatile properties to smoke, grill, braise and kitchen oven, Wood Pellet Smoker and Grill can be used to cook endless dishes and recipes. In fact, there is no actual limit to the recipes you can cook like hot dogs, chicken, vegetables, seafood, rabbit,

ken, brisket, turkey and even more. The cooking
cess is very easy; all you have to do is to pack your
rite wood pellets into the hopper; then program
temperature you desire on the controller; then
e the food on the pellet Smoker and Grill. That is,
d the pellet will be able to maintain the tempera-
and keep the pellets burning.

t Smoker and Grills are characterized by being
tric and it requires a usual standard outlet of
ut 110v so that you can power the digital board,
and auger.

e is a wide variety of types of pellet smokers and
like electric pellet smokers, wood fired grills,

wood pellet grills and wood pellet smokers; to name
a few pellet Smoker and Grill names. But all these
names refer to the same outdoor cooker appliance
that is only fueled by hardwood pellets. And there are
many brands of Wood Pellet Smoker and Grills, like
Traeger.

For instance, Traeger is known for being one of the
world's most well-known brands of pellet grills. Indeed,
Joe Traeger was the person who invented the pellet
grill during the mid-1980s, and he gave his name to
this invention. And when the Traeger patent expired,
many other Pellet Smoker and Grills came to life into
the market.

MY SHOPPING TIPS!

PELLET GRILLS

Traeger Pellet Grills: https://amzn.to/3rC8wX6

Traeger Grills Ranger Grill: https://amzn.to/3tJhi7x

ACCESSORIES

Traeger Pellet Grill Cover: https://amzn.to/3aGg0Bu

Traeger Pellet Sensor: https://amzn.to/2MOskYD

Traeger Pellet Folding Shelf: https://amzn.to/3cWALvM

Cooking Gloves: https://amzn.to/3aTDzXY

The Original Turkey Injector: https://amzn.to/3q5b0x0

Set of 5 Disposable Aluminum Wood-Fired Cooking: https://amzn.to/3tFz77E

WOOD PELLETS

Traeger Grills PEL331 Signature Blend Grill: https://amzn.to/2YWogYM

Green Mountain Grills Premium Apple: https://amzn.to/2YZdQHU

Chapter 1.

THE FUNDAMENTALS OF SMOKING

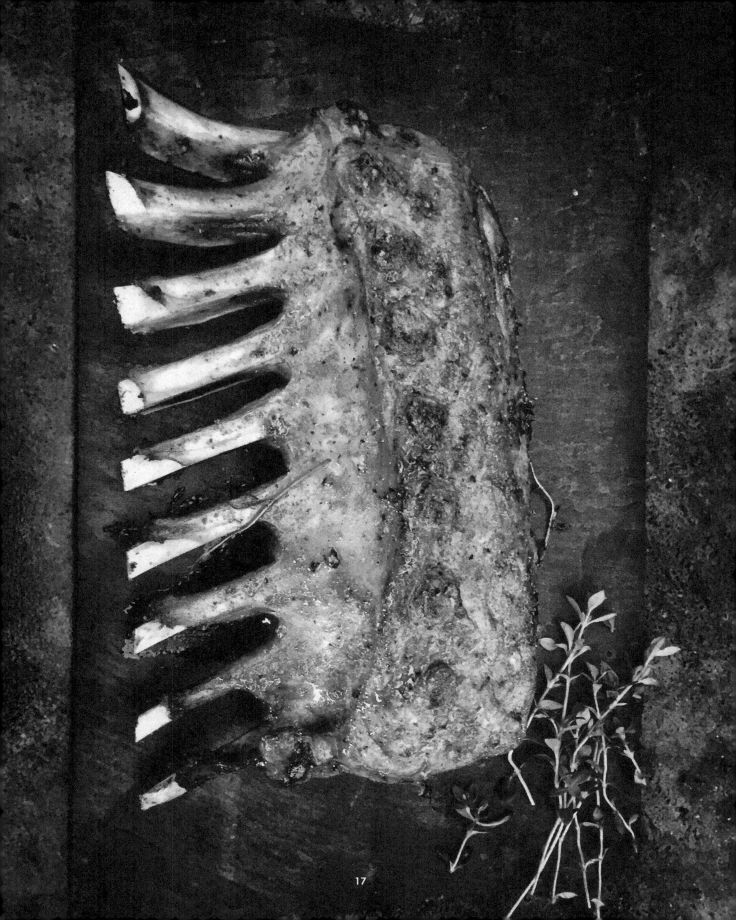

WHAT IS WOOD PELLET SMOKERS GRILL?

A pellet grill is essentially a multi-functional grill that has been so designed that the compressed wood pellets end up being the real source of fuel. They are outdoor cookers and tend to combine the different striking elements of smokers, gas grills, ovens, and even charcoal. The very reason which has cemented their popularity for ages have to be the kind of quality and flavor that they tend to infuse in the food you make on them.

Not only this, by varying the kind of wood pellet you are using, but you can also bring in the variation in the actual flavor of the food as well. Often, the best chefs use a mix and match technique of wood pellets to infuse the food with their signature flavor that have people hooked to their cooking in no time.

The clinical definition of a wood pellet smoker grill is smoking, grilling, roasting, and baking barbecue using compressed hardwood sawdust such as apple, cherry, hickory, maple, mesquite, oak, and other wood pellets. It is a pit. Wood pellet smoker grills provide the flavor profile and moisture that only hardwood dishes can achieve. Depending on the manufacturer and model, the grill temperature on many models can be well over 150 ° F to 600 ° F. Gone are the days when people say they cannot bake on wood pellet smoking grills!

Wood pellet smoker grills offer the succulence, convenience, and safety not found in charcoal or gas grills. The smoke here is not as thick as other smokers common to you. Its design provides the versatility and benefits of a convection oven. A wood pellet smoker grill is safe and easy to operate.

HOW DO THEY WORK?

The grill would run on electricity and therefore it needs to be plugged in for the sake of deriving power.

The design is such that pellets have to be added to the hopper that in turn will funnel down owing to the presence of a rotating auger and a motor.

The auger aims to make sure that the pellets get pushed down to the fire pot at the pre-configured speed which is determined by the yard control panel showing the temperature. As soon as the pellets reach the fire pot, there is an ignition rod that creates a flame that in turn causes the production of smoke.

Also, a fan is present at the bottom which helps in pushing both the generated heat and smoke upwards on the grill and thereby allows for the convection style of even cooking.

This happens to be the basic mechanism of the working of a wood pellet grill. Knowing the different parts of the wood pellet grill and also the working mechanism will prepare you in a much better way to ensure that you can use the grill in the right manner.

However, before we venture further into the recipes, we are going to shift our focus on some important points about these grills. This is because the right knowledge is crucial to ensuring that you know what you are getting into.

HOW TO PICK THE BEST WOOD PELLETS

What makes a wood pellet smoker and grill unique is the very thing that fuels it -- wood pellets. Wood pellets are compressed sawdust, made from either pine wood, birch wood, fir wood, or crop stalks. Culinary-wise, wood pellets are used mostly as fuel for pellet smokers and grills, although they can also be used for household heating. What makes wood pellets for cooking special, though, is that they come in flavors. And speaking of flavors, here is a quick wood pellet flavor guide for you:

Apple & Cherry Pellets: These pellets possess a smoky, mild, sweet flavor. They can enhance mild meat and are usually the go-to flavor for cooking pork or poultry. Despite being able to produce great smoke, these pellets are very mild.

Alder Pellets: This type of pellet is mild and neutral, but with some sweetness in it. If you're looking for something that provides a good amount of smoke but won't overpower delicate meat like chicken and fish, this is the flavor to go to.

Hickory Pellets: Hickory pellets produce a rich, Smokey, and bacon-like flavor. These are the pellets that are widely used for barbecue. Since this type of pellet is rich and Smokey, it can tend to be overwhelming. If that is the case, consider mixing it with apple or oak pellets.

Maple Pellets: If you are looking for something that is mild and comes with a hint of sweetness, maple pellets are the best option for you. They are great to use on turkey or pork.

Mesquite Pellets: A favorite option for Texas BBQ, mesquite pellets are characterized by a strong, spicy, and tangy flavor.

Oak Pellets: Oak pellets come in between apple and hickory. They are a bit stronger than the former and a bit milder than the latter and are an excellent choice when you're cooking fish or vegetables.

Pecan Pellets: Pecan is an all-time favorite. It's very similar to Hickory, but with a touch of vanilla, nutty flavor. The perfect pellets for beef and chicken, pecan pellets are very palatable and suits all occasions.

COOKING TEMPERATURES, TIMES, AND DONENESS

With so many recipes to try with your pellet grill, it is easy to get overwhelmed right away. One important thing to keep in mind is that lower temperatures produce smoke, while higher temperatures do not. Follow this useful guide below to know the temperature and time it requires to get the perfectly flavored meat each time.

• Beef briskets are best cooked at 250 degrees using the smoke setting for at least 4 hours by itself and covered with foil for another 4 hours.

• Pork ribs should be cooked at 275 degrees on the smoke setting for 3 hours and covered with foil for another 2-3 hours.

• Steaks require 400-450 degrees for about 10 minutes on each side.

• Turkey can be cooked at 375 degrees for 20 minutes per pound of meat. For smoked turkey, the heat settings should be around 180-225 degrees for 10-12 hours or until the inside of the turkey reaches 165 degrees.

• Chicken breasts can be cooked at 400-450 degrees for 15 minutes on each side.

• A whole chicken cooks at 400-450 degrees for 1.5 hours or until the internal temperature reaches 165 degrees.

• Bacon and sausage can be cooked at 425 degrees for 5-8 minutes on each side.

• Hamburgers should be cooked at 350 degrees for at least 8 minutes for each side.

• You can smoke salmon for 1-1.5 hours and finish with a high setting for 2-3 minutes on each side.

• Shrimps cook at 400-450 degrees for 3-5 minutes on each side. If you prefer a smokier flavor, set the temperature at 225 degrees for about 30 minutes.

ACCESSORIES NEEDED

You're off to a great start with your pellet grill, but there are a few other valuable tools that are well worthwhile to invest in. These tools appear throughout this cookbook – some are vital, and some simply elevate your repertoire.

Probe Meat Thermometer – If your grill doesn't have probe thermometers built-in, you 100% need to get one or two of them. They are crucial to almost any recipe, but especially for smoking recipes. Measuring your meat's internal temperature is the only way you can know when your food is safely cooked all the way through. It will also help you pull your food off of the cooker at your exact desired doneness.

BBQ Gloves – For your safety, it's best to have a pair of BBQ gloves just in case. Most of our recipes don't require BBQ gloves to safely handle your food, but some do. Plus, it never hurts to take extra caution when you're dealing with scorching hot temperatures.

Silicone Basting Brush – Many grill and smoker recipes utilize marinades that need to be brushed or basted onto your food. Basting brushes are quite affordable and a borderline necessity for any grilling toolbox.

Cast Iron Skillet – The cast iron skillet is one of the most versatile pans in any kitchen, and since pellet grills can bake, roast, and braise, we'll use them on the pellet grill too.

HOW TO CLEAN YOUR GRILL

Just like every appliance, keeping your smoker clean is essential as well. If you neglect your appliance, it might slowly accumulate debris, oil, and drips, which might ultimately result in the appliance getting damaged.

The good idea is to keep a mixture of mild dish detergent and warm water handy as they are perfect when it comes to cleaning smokers. Alternatively, you may use non-abrasive cleaners as well should you choose.

A good tip is to clean your Smoker after every smoking session to avoid having a massive clean-up session down the road.

That being said, let me break down the necessary steps of cleaning your Smoker

Steps for cleaning the Smoker after every use:

• If you have used Wood Chips, make sure first to empty your smoker box and discard any ash. Carefully wipe the side of the box with a damp rag

• Next, remove the cooking racks, water pan, drip tray pan and wash them with warm soapy water, rinse and dry them

• As an added to apply a gentle coat of vegetable oil over the racks before your next smoking session for mess-free Smoking

• Remove the meat probe and clean it with a damp cloth as well

• Wipe the door seal with a damp cloth and get rid of any debris or residue

• Allow your Smoker to dry up before using again completely

Steps to keeping the outside of your Smoker clean

• Gently wipe the control panel on the top of your Smoker using a damp cloth with warm water, wipe it dry

• If your model has a window, then use approved cleaners suitable for ceramic glass cooktops to clean both the inside and outside of the window

Steps to cleaning the thermostats (If your device has it):

• Carefully wipe the surface of the two thermostats located on the reading inside of the wall of your Smoker using a soft, damp cloth

• Make sure to dip the cloth in warm soapy water before wiping, let them dry once done

Steps for cleaning the inside of your Smoker

• Make sure that your Smoker is wholly cooled off

• Take out the racks, water pan, drip tray, and smoker box

• Take a small brush/towel and brush any debris alongside the bottom and upper part of the Smoker

• Wipe any residue out of the chamber

• Use warm soapy water and carefully scrub the interior surfaces of the Smoker using a plastic bristle brush, wipe it dry once done

Chapter 2.

BENEFITS OF THE WOOD PELLET SMOKER-GRILL

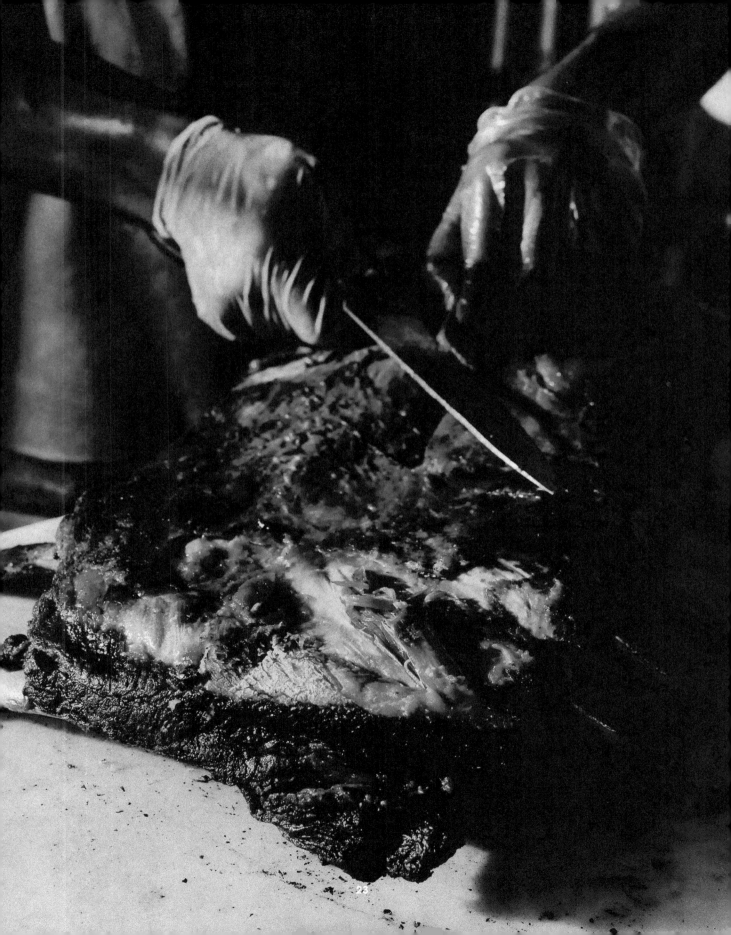

There are several advantages to using a wood pellet smoker-grill. Not only does it enhance the taste of your food, but it also offers several other benefits. Here are some of the biggest benefits of a wood pellet smoker-grill!

SAVES TIME

It is a no-brainer that anything that saves time as well as effort, especially when it comes to cooking, deserves a warm welcome. One of the biggest advantages of using wood pellet grills is that they save you a lot of time. You can make your smoked dishes much faster and with much more ease and comfort. You can pre-heat them quickly, so you will save a lot of time.

OFFERS VARIED COOKING OPTIONS

The best thing about wood pellet smoker-grills is that they give you several options for easy cooking. They are versatile and let you easily experiment with recipes and food. You can try various smoked recipes on the grill and enjoy healthy cooking. The versatility of pellet grills is probably one of their best qualities. This ensures that you can enjoy several lip-smacking recipes in a matter of minutes. In addition, you can use pellet grills for cooking all kinds of food, from braised short ribs to chicken wings.

OFFERS VARIETY

Another significant advantage of using a wood pellet smoker-grill is that these smokers and grills come in a plethora of sizes and shapes. These grills are built and designed keeping the preferences, needs, and tastes of customers in mind. Therefore, people who are looking for convenient cooking tools can always find something for themselves in wood pellet smokers and grills. You can also choose from a wide range of flavors, such as maple, pecan, hickory, apple, and much more.

COLD SMOKING

In addition to wood pellet fire grills and smokers, you can buy cold smokers from some companies. You can cook salmon and cheese dishes in these cold smokers.

EASE OF USE

It is common to see many people get intimidated by the idea of using a pellet grill. However, those fears are unfounded. While a pellet grill is quite different from your standard charcoal grills or gas grills, they are surprisingly easy to use. These grills come with controls that users can set and then simply forget about. They come with several features that make the entire process of grilling a piece of cake.

These grills usually do not require any lighter fluid and they start with a single button. In addition, irrespective of the weather or the temperature outside, these grills can keep the temperature within a 10-degree range of your set temperature. This allows you to cook with zero effort like a pro. These grills are also designed to ensure that you do not overcook or over-smoke your food. Plus, they never flare-up. So, there is no need for you to worry about your beautiful eyebrows.

VALUE

While pellet smokers are slightly more expensive than standard grills, this is for a good reason. As mentioned above, these pieces of equipment offer the perfect combination of a smoker and a grill. They come with solid construction and stainless-steel components. This is precisely why they also come with a nice four-year warranty.

This means that you will not buy these grills for sum-

mer only to dispose of them come winter. In addition, fuel efficiency is another one of their advantages. They come packed with double-wall insulation, which helps them sustain their temperatures better as well as use less fuel.

So, what are you waiting for? If you like to smoke or grill your food, it is not possible to go wrong with a good-quality pellet grill. They provide a wide range of advantages, such as their ease of use and the incredible flavor of your favorite smoked wood. Therefore, these grills are an amazing value for the money.

Keeping this in mind, let us dive right into some amazing tried-and-tested recipes using a wood pellet smoker-grill!

KNOW YOUR MEAT

Choose the type of meat that tastes good with a smoky flavor. Following meat goes well for smoking.

Beef: ribs, brisket, and corned beef.

Pork: spareribs, roast, shoulder, and ham.

Poultry: whole chicken, a whole turkey, and big game hens.

Seafood: Salmon, scallops, trout, and lobster.

Getting Meat Ready

Prepare meat according to the recipe. Sometimes meat is cured, marinated, or simply seasoned with the rub. These preparation methods ensure smoked meat turns out flavorful, tender, and extremely juicy.

Brine is a solution to treating poultry, pork, or ham. It involves dissolving brine ingredients in water poured into a huge container and then adding meat to it. Then let soak for at least 8 hours and after that, rinse it well and pat dry before you begin smoking.

Marinate treat beef or briskets and add flavors to it. It's better to make deep cuts in meat to let marinate ingredients deep into it. Drain meat or smoke it straightaway.

Rubs are commonly used to treat beef, poultry, or ribs. They are a combination of salt and many spices, rubbed generously all over the meat. Then the meat is left to rest for at least 2 hours or more before smoking it.

Before smoking meat, make sure it is at room tempe-rature. This ensures the meat is cooked evenly and reaches its internal temperature at the end of the smoking time.

PLACING MEAT IN THE SMOKER

Do not place the meat directly overheat into the smoker because the main purpose of smoking is cooking meat at low temperatures. Set aside your fuel on one side of the smoker and place the meat on the other side and let cook.

Smoking time: The smoking time of meat depends on the internal temperature. For this, use a meat thermometer and insert it into the thickest part of the meat. The smoking time also varies with the size of the meat. Check recipes to determine the exact smoking time for the meat.

BASTING MEAT

Some recipes call for brushing the meat with thin solutions, sauces, or marinade. This step not only makes meat better in taste, but also helps to maintain moisture in meat through the smoking process. Read the recipe to check out if basting is necessary.

Taking out meat: When the meat reaches its desired internal temperature, remove it from the smoker. Generally, poultry should be removed from the smoker when its internal temperature reaches 165 degrees F. For ground meats, ham, and pork, the internal temperature should be 160 degrees F. 145 degrees F is the internal temperature for chops, roast, and steaks.

KNOW YOUR FISH

1. Choose Salmon, Swordfish, Tuna, Mahi-Mahi, Halibut, or Snapper

2. If you can't get fresh, look for "Frozen-At-Sea."

Your grilled fish recipe is only as good as your fish is fresh. If you're buying fresh, your local fishmonger or high-quality seafood grocer can give you fillets or steaks that should be firm to the touch and have a clean ocean smell. If your fish smells fishy in more ways than one, put it down and run away. Another alternative is to choose fish that is "Frozen at Sea." This can sometimes be better quality than fresh fish if you don't live near the water.

PREPPING YOUR FISH AND GRILL

3. Remove any pin bones, if your fishmonger hasn't already

These little bones can be pretty pesky while you're eating. To remove them, gently rub your fingers over the flesh. Pin bones will slightly poke out of the surface and are often located in the middle, meatiest part of the fish. You can easily remove them using needle-nose pliers.

4. Cook on clean and oiled grill grates

Clean your cooking grids to get great contact between your fish and the piping hot metal. In addition, the oil will season the cooking surface and prevent your masterpiece from sticking to the grids. Trust us, there's nothing worse than a perfectly grilled fish that ends up stuck to the cooking grids.

Add your high-smoke point oils, like canola, sunflower, or safflower - by using a spray, a paper towel, or rubbing the oil on an onion, and then rubbing the onion on the cooking surface.

5. Wait until your grill is nice and hot before you begin cooking

Most recipes will call for a medium to high temperature of 400°F to 450°F Letting the grill come up to temp prior to cooking will reduce the chance of sticking and shorten overall cook time

FISH COOKING TIPS

6. Grill using a foil packet

This is a foolproof method for easy cooking and amazing flavor. Foil packets also work particularly well for delicate fish that flake apart. Fold the foil so it creates a pouch to hold liquids and add in your fish, as well as, all your favorite flavors, like citrus, vinegar, soy sauce, olive oil, and other seasonings and rubs.

7. Wood Plank Grilling

Cedar planking is another surprisingly easy and fun to cook right on the grates. It also infuses hardwood flavor directly into the fish. Just be sure to soak the plank from 1 to 4 hours, prior to grilling. For an added touch, you can let both sides of the plank char and smolder for a minute prior to laying the fish on it to cook.

8. Add olive oil, or mayo if grilling fillets or steaks right on the grates

Mayo is an underrated, golden secret to deliciously grilled fish. It has a ton of oil and flavor. Mixed in with a few spices, it serves as the perfect pre and post grilling marinade. Just add a little of that or some go-to olive oil to both sides before searing.

9. Flip only once

Flipping only once, is another key to prevent your fish from falling apart. You know that it's time to flip when you see a nice brown crust on the outside.

A good rule of thumb is, 8 minutes of total grilling time, per 1 inch of thickness. So, look for signs to turn a 1-inch fillet or steak after 3-4 minutes.

FISH COOKING TIPS

10. Fish that's cooked properly should be opaque and flake easily

Fish can be tricky to track if it's covered in sauce or in a foil packet. However, when it comes to learning how to grill fish, it's important to know that overcooking fish is just as bad as overcooking anything else. It becomes dry or loses rich flavor and texture. Therefore, if you're not using an instant-read thermometer, it's totally ok to pull the fish off a little early to check that it's done to your liking

11. It's better to remove your fish a little early, rather than a little late

Fish can be tricky to track if it's covered in sauce or in a foil packet. However, when it comes to learning how to grill fish, it's important to know that overcooking fish is just as bad as overcooking anything else. It becomes dry or loses rich flavor and texture. Therefore, if you're not using an instant-read thermometer, it's totally ok to pull the fish off a little early to check that it's done to your liking

Chapter 3.

GAME MEAT

384 SMOKED VENISON AND BOAR

Preparation Time: 5 minutes	Cooking Time: 5 hours	Servings: 6

Ingredients

1 lb of ground wild boar

1 lb of ground venison

2 Teaspoons of celery salt

2 Teaspoons of red pepper flakes

Directions:

1. Start your Wood Pellet Smoker with the lid open for about 4 to 5 minutes and keep the temperature on smoke

2. Combine all your ingredients in a bowl and form bars from the meat with your hand

3. Place the bars on the grill grate and smoke for about 4 to 5 hours

4. Remove from the grill and let cool for about 5 minutes

5. Serve and enjoy your dish!

Nutrition:

Calories: 134,

Fat: 6g,

Carbohydrates: 0g,

Dietary Fiber: 0 g,

Protein: 18g

385. SMOKED WHOLE DUCK

Preparation Time: 15 minutes	Cooking Time: 2 hours	Servings: 4

Ingredients:

2 Tablespoons of baking soda

1 Tablespoon of Chinese five spices

1 Thawed duck

1 Granny smith cored and diced apple

1 Quartered sliced orange

2 Tablespoons of chicken seasoning, divided

Directions:

1. Start by washing the duck under cool running water from the inside and out; then pat the meat dry with clean paper towels

2. Combine the Chicken seasoning and the Chinese Five spice together; then combine with the baking soda for extra crispy skin

3. Season the duck from the inside and out

4. Tuck the apple and the orange and apple slices into the cavity.

5. Turn your Wood Pellet Smoker Grill to smoke model; then let the fire catch and set it to about 300°F to preheat

6. Place the duck on the grill grate or in a pan; then roast for about 2 ½ hours at a temperature of about 160°F

7. Place the foil loosely on top of the duck and let rest for about 15 minutes.

8. Serve and enjoy your delicious dish!

Nutrition:

Calories: 157,

Fat: 10g,

Carbohydrates: 10g,

Dietary Fiber: 1.3 g,

Protein: 11.1g

386. SMOKED VENISON

Preparation Time: 10 minutes	Cooking Time: 2 hours	Servings: 4

Ingredients

1 lb of venison tenderloin

¼ Cup of lemon juice

¼ Cup of olive oil

5 Minced garlic cloves

1 Teaspoon of salt

1 Teaspoon of ground black pepper

Directions:

1. Start by putting the whole venison tenderloin, in a zip-style bag or in a large bowl.

2. Add the lemon juice, the olive oil, the garlic, the salt and the pepper into a food processor

3. Process your ingredients until they are very well incorporated

4. Pour the marinade on top of the venison; then massage it in very well

5. Refrigerate and let marinate for about 4 hours or for an overnight

6. When you are ready to cook; just remove the venison from your marinade, and rinse it off very well.

7. Pat the meat dry and let it come to the room temperature for about 30 minutes before cooking it

8. In the meantime, preheat your smoker to a temperature of about 225°F

9. Smoke the tenderloin for about 2 hours

10. Let the meat rest for about 10 minutes before slicing it

11. Top with black pepper; then serve and enjoy your dish!

Nutrition:

Calories: 300,
Fat: 17g,
Carbohydrates: 3g,
Dietary Fiber: 0g,
Protein: 33g

387. VENISON MEATLOAF

Preparation Time: 20 minutes	Cooking Time: 1 1/2 hours	Servings: 5

Ingredients

2 lbs of ground venison

1 Diced onion

1 Beaten egg

1 Pinch of salt

1 Pinch of pepper

1 Tablespoons of Worcestershire sauce

1 Cup of bread crumbs

1 Oz of packet onion soup mix

1 Cup of milk

For the glaze topping

¼ Cup of ketchup

¼ Cup of brown sugar

¼ Cup of apple cider vinegar

Directions:

1. When you are ready to cook, start your wood pellet grill on smoke with the lid open for about 4 to 5 minutes

2. Set the temperature to about 350°F and preheat with the lid close for about 10 to 15 minutes

3. Spray a loaf pan with cooking spray; then in a large bowl combine altogether the ground venison with the onion, the egg, the salt, the pepper and the breadcrumbs

4. Add the Worcestershire sauce, the milk, and the onion soup packet and be careful not to over mix.

5. In a small bowl, mix the ketchup, the brown sugar and the apple cider vinegar.

6. Spread half of the glaze on the bottom and the sides of the pan; then add the meatloaf and spread the remaining quantity on top of the meatloaf

7. Directly place on the smoker grill grate and smoke for about 1 hour and 15 minutes

8. Let the meatloaf cool for several minutes before slicing it

9. Serve and enjoy your dish!

Nutrition:

Calories: 219,
Fat: 15g,
Carbohydrates: 0.8g,
Dietary Fiber: 0.3g,
Protein: 30g

388. WOOD PELLET ELK JERKY

| Preparation Time: 10 minutes | Cooking Time: 6 hours | Servings: 10 |

Ingredients

4 Pounds of elk hamburger

¼ Cup of soy sauce

¼ Cup of Teriyaki sauce

¼ Cup of Worcestershire sauce

1 Tablespoon of paprika

1 Tablespoon of chili powder

1 Tablespoon of crushed red pepper

3 Tablespoons of hot sauce

1 Tablespoon of pepper

1 Tablespoon of garlic powder

1 Tablespoon of onion salt

1 Tablespoon of salt

Directions:

1. Start by mixing all of the ingredients of the seasoning and the elk hamburger in a large bowl; then let sit in the refrigerator for about 12 hours

2. Light your wood pellet smoker to a low temperature of about 160°F

3. Take the elk meat out of your refrigerator and start making strips of the meat manually or with a rolling pin

4. Add smoker wood chips to your wood pellet smoker grill and rub some quantity of olive oil over the smoker grate lay out the strips in one row

5. Warm a dehydrator up about half way during the smoking process

6. Remove the elk jerky meat off your smoker at about 3 hours

7. Line it into the kitchen.

8. Line your dehydrator with the elk jerky meat and keep it in for about 5 to 6 additional hours

9. Serve and enjoy!

Nutrition:

389. GAME MEAT RACKS

| Preparation Time: 15 minutes | Cooking Time: 30 minutes | Servings: 4 |

Ingredients

500 g of game minced meat (leg, shoulder of stag or roe deer)

100 ml milk (lukewarm)

100 g bacon cubes

1 teaspoon mustard (medium hot)

3 shallots

2 cloves of garlic

2 juniper berries

2 sprig (s) of thyme

2 sprig (s) of rosemary

1 roll (from the day before)

1 egg

Salt

Pepper

Rapeseed oil

Directions:

1. Debark the bread and dice it. Pour the milk over it and let it steep for 10 minutes.

2. Peel and chop the shallots and garlic.

3. Sweat the bacon, shallots and garlic in 1 tablespoon of rapeseed oil, allow cooling a little. Finely grind the juniper berries. Pluck the thyme and rosemary and chop finely.

4. Mix the minced meat with the roll, bacon mixture, juniper berries, mustard, egg and the herbs and season with salt and pepper.

5. Shape the mixture into 8 even labels and cover them in the refrigerator for about 1 hour.

6. Prepare grill for direct and indirect heat (200 ° C). If a charcoal grill (57) is used, you need a 2/3 full chimney with glowed briquettes.

7. Spray the hot grate with anti-stick spray and grill the labels directly on both sides for 2-3 minutes. Then position it indirectly and continue grilling until a core temperature of 65 ° C is reached. Tip

8. If there is not enough time to cool the Laberl for 1 hour, you can freeze them for 15 minutes.

Nutrition:

Calories: 150,

Fat: 15g,

Carbohydrates: 29g,

Dietary Fiber: 1.3 g,

Protein: 11.1g

390. ALL AMERICAN BBQ SPARE RIBS

| Preparation Time: 15 minutes | Cooking Time: 2 hours | Servings: 8 |

Ingredients

2 racks of grill, 2.75 kg of skinned pork ribs

2 to 3 tbsp chicken seasoning

1 cup of apple juice, cider or beer

50 g barbecue sauce

Directions:

1. Remove the silver skin part on the back of the ribs (Indian I butcher said not yet). Said would prevent the penetration of the herbs and smoke.

2. Sprinkle the chicken seasoning on both sides of the ribs. When you are ready to cook, start the Traeger grill on SMOKE with the lid open until there is a good fire (4 to 5 minutes).

3. Increase the temperature to 95 ° C and preheat with the lid closed for 10 to 15 minutes. Arrange the ribs on the racks or grid, with the bones down. Cook for 3 to 4 hours. After 1 hour, spray with call juice. Repeat said after every hour of cooking. After 3 to 4 hours of cooking, rub the ribs with the barbecue sauce. Grill for another 30 minutes to 1 hour, cut into individual ribs and serve with extra barbecue sauce.

Nutrition:

Calories: 157,
Fat: 10g,
Carbohydrates: 10g,
Dietary Fiber: 1.3 g,
Protein: 11.1g

391. FRIED POULTRY OR GAME WITH GARNISH

| Preparation Time: 10 minutes | Cooking Time: 2 hours | Servings: 4 |

Ingredients

250 g chicken, or 250 g turkey, or 1/4 pheasant, 2/3 hazel grouse or gray partridge

6 g butter

25 g mayonnaise with gherkins

Lettuce leaves or parsley (for garnish) (optional)

150 g ready-made garnish of green lettuce leaves, pickled cucumbers, red cabbage, Provencal cabbage, pickled tomatoes, pickled apples and pears

Salt

Directions:

1. Chilled fried poultry is cut into portions. Hazel grouse and partridge are used whole or carcasses are cut in half (see the materials "Features of frying poultry and game" and "Refueling of poultry and game").

2. Pieces of poultry or game are placed on a dish, garnished with bouquets of green lettuce, pickled cucumbers, red cabbage, Provencal cabbage, pickled tomatoes, as well as pickled pears and apples (see the recipe "Sauerkraut Salad (Provencal)").

3. On top, the dish is additionally decorated with salad leaves or parsley sprigs. Separately, mayonnaise with gherkins is served in a gravy boat (see "Sauce mayonnaise with gherkins").

4. Recommendations

5. Read about the properties of apples, butter, red cabbage and white cabbage in the articles "Apples", "Butter", "Red cabbage", "White cabbage (fresh)".

Nutrition:

Calories: 176,
Fat: 10g,
Carbohydrates: 10g,
Dietary Fiber: 1.3 g,
Protein: 11.1g

392. GUINEA FOWL STUFFED WITH VEGETABLES

Preparation Time: 10 minutes

Cooking Time: 2 hours

Servings: 5

Ingredients

1 guinea fowl

2 shallots

13 cloves of garlic

20 g parsley

Salt

Olive oil

10 onions cut into quarters

5 large potatoes cut into quarters

3 pickled tomatoes

4 fresh or canned tomatoes (skinless and cut into quarters)

Fresh thyme

200 g chicken broth or broth from any other poultry

20-30 g butter

Ground black pepper

Directions:

1. Stuff the guinea fowl with 2 shallots, 3 cloves of garlic, a slice of butter, thyme and chopped parsley. Outside, pepper and salt the guinea fowl.

2. Put the stuffed guinea fowl in a cast-iron roaster and fry on all sides in a large amount of olive oil. After that, take out the guinea fowl from the gosper and put it aside temporarily, and fry the potatoes, onions and garlic cloves in olive oil. Add chopped tomatoes (both) to vegetables. Put thyme, salt and ground pepper here. Pour in 100 g of broth. Place the guinea fowl on a layer of vegetables.

3. Place the roaster in an oven preheated to 170 degrees. Keep the guinea fowl there for 75 minutes. Moreover, every 15 minutes it is necessary to water the guinea fowl from above with the remaining broth.

Nutrition:

Calories: 157,
Fat: 18g,
Carbohydrates: 17g,
Dietary Fiber: 1.3 g,
Protein: 15.1g

393. PARTRIDGE WITH CABBAGE

Preparation Time: 15 minutes

Cooking Time: 50 minutes

Servings: 4

Ingredients

1 kg of white cabbage (1 small head of cabbage)

2 partridges

200 g tea sausage

15 g smoked brisket

50 g butter

2 carrots

2 onions

2 carnation buds

Salt

Ground black pepper

15 g parsley

Water

Directions:

1. Cut the head of cabbage into 4 parts. Remove the stump and thick ribs. Then immerse the cabbage in boiling salted water for 2 minutes. Then remove the cabbage from the boiling water, rinse with cold water, place the cabbage in a colander and let the water drain.

2. Brown the partridges in oil in a frying pan, then salt and pepper.

3. Put chopped cabbage and carrots, sprigs of greens, as well as 2 onions in a pressure cooker (or a rooster), in each of which first stick 1 clove bud. After that, pour 125 g of boiling water into a pressure cooker (or gosper), add salt and pepper. Bring out the contents of the cooker to a boil with the lid open.

4. Place the sautéed partridge pieces in a pressure cooker (or gosper). Add finely chopped sausage and brisket there. Close the pressure cooker (or goose maker) with a lid and simmer the partridges in the pressure cooker for 30 minutes, and in the goose maker for 1 hour.

Nutrition:

Calories: 187,
Fat: 10g,
Carbohydrates: 10g,
Dietary Fiber: 1.3 g,
Protein: 11.1g

394. RECIPE SPARE RIBS

Preparation Time: 15 minutes	Cooking Time: 2 hours	Servings: 4

Ingredients spareribs

1500 grams spareribs

2 tablespoons mustard

3 tablespoons Mother of all rubs

4 tablespoons Cola BBQ Sauce

25 grams butter

Supplies

4 aluminum containers

BBQ with lid

2 chunks smoking wood apple

Aluminum foil

Nutrition:

Calories: 167,

Fat: 20g,

Carbohydrates: 24g,

Dietary Fiber: 1.3 g,

Protein: 12.1g

Directions:

1. Rinse the ribs well, pat them dry and remove the fleece. Make sure you use a handy knife for this (no sharp point). Make an opening by sliding the knife between the fleeces and carefully unravel the fleece.

2. Use your fingers for this, but you can also use the knife. Make sure you don't damage the meat itself by running your knife only along the bone (and not along the meat).

3. Cut off loose pieces of meat and fat at the top and cut the ribs in half.

4. Coat the bottom with mustard and sprinkle with half of the rub. Flip the ribs and grease the top with mustard as well and sprinkle with the other half of the rub.

5. Prepare the BBQ for indirect grilling at a temperature of 110 degrees. Add the smoking wood to the coals as soon as the BBQ is up to temperature.

6. Place the ribs on the BBQ (the indirect part) and smoke the ribs for about an hour.

7. Place the ribs all in a separate aluminum container, add a small knob of butter and wrap the containers tightly with aluminum foil so that no more air can reach.

8. Place the ribs in the trays on the BBQ for another two hours.

9. Remove the ribs from the containers and place them on the wire rack on the indirect part for another 20 minutes and brush the ribs with barbecue sauce.

10. Ready and enjoy!

11. Tip!

12. For anyone who prefers not to eat pork, you can also replace the spare ribs with veal spare ribs. These are slightly less fat, but also have a very tasty taste.

395. QUAIL ON THE GRILL MARINATED WITH VINEGAR AND ONIONS

Preparation Time: 15 minutes	Cooking Time: 1 1/2 hours	Servings: 6

Ingredients:

Quail - 4 pcs.

For the marinade:

Onions - 2 pcs.

Vinegar (9%) - 30 ml

Salt to taste

Ground black pepper - to taste

Garlic - 1 clove.

Directions:

1. Wash quail carcasses under running cold water, dry on paper towels and put on a cutting board with the backup.

2. Using kitchen scissors, cut each quail along the back, unfold the ribs to the sides and lay the carcass breast up. Beat the carcass lightly with a meat hammer (you can use the handle of a knife instead of a hammer).

3. For the marinade, peel and cut onions into several pieces. Fold in a blender and puree with a clove of garlic.

4. In a separate bowl, mix the vinegar with 50 ml of cold water.

5. Place the quail carcasses in a suitable bowl or food container, shifting with onion and garlic gruel, sprinkle with salt and pepper to taste. Stir it well so that the meat is well covered with the onion mass on all sides.

6. Pour diluted vinegar over the quail, stir, put a little oppression and put in the refrigerator for at least 2-3 hours, or better overnight.

7. Burn firewood in the grill to the "gray" coals. Grease the sieve with vegetable oil, lay the quail carcasses, laying them out, as shown in the photo. Remember to shake off all the onions from them.

8. Bake over glowing coals, turning the wire rack from one side to the other from time to time. The quails on the wire rack are ready in about 20 minutes. Their readiness can be easily checked by piercing the breast with a knife: if clear juice flows out without impurities of blood, then the meat can be removed from the barbecue. Transfer the finished quails to a dish, cover with foil and let them rest for another 20 minutes. Then you can serve it with fresh vegetables, herbs and sauce to taste. Enjoy your meal!

Nutrition:

Calories: 186,

Fat: 10g,

Carbohydrates: 21g,

Dietary Fiber: 1.3 g,

Protein: 11.1g

396. FILET MIGNON WITH BERNESE SAUCE

Preparation Time: 10 minutes	Cooking Time: 45 minutes	Servings: 4

Ingredients

- 1/3 cup white vinegar
- 1/3 cup dry white wine
- 1 teaspoon of pepper
- 1 teaspoon minced shallot
- 2 teaspoons chopped parsley
- 1/4 of teaspoon of tarragon
- 3 pieces of egg yolk
- 4 pieces of beef fillet 2 cm thick
- 1 pinch of salt

Directions:

1. Combine wine, vinegar, pepper, shallots and tarragon, heat and reduce to have 1/3 cup. Strain it and reserve.

2. Put a bowl on a water bath, the yolks and the vinegar mixture and heat moving with a balloon whisk to begin to thicken, then put the parsley and remove from heat immediately and set aside.

3. Heat the grill and when it is very hot put a little oil and seal the fillets on the 2 sides, to brown a little and put salt and pepper.

4. Once the steaks are well cooked. Serve immediately with the Bernese sauce.

Nutrition:

Calories: 157,
Fat: 10g,
Carbohydrates: 10g,
Dietary Fiber: 1.3 g,
Protein: 11.1g

397. WILD ELK TENDERLOIN KABOBS

Preparation Time: 15 minutes	Cooking Time: 15 minutes	Servings: 8

Ingredients

- 3 lb elk tenderloin, cut into 2-inch chunks
- 3 tbsp balsamic vinegar
- 3 tbsp olive oil
- 3 yellow squash, whole
- 3 zucchini, whole
- 12 sweet peppers, small
- 12 cherry tomatoes
- 2 tbsp Traeger prime rib rub

Directions:

1. Drizzle elk tenderloin chunks with vinegar and oil then let sit in a bowl, large.

2. Meanwhile, chop squash and zucchini into ¾ -inch thick coins.

3. Now cut ends off from the peppers and remove seeds.

4. Place peppers, tomatoes, zucchini, and squash coins to the bowl with tenderloin then toss them. Add more vinegar and oil until everything is lightly coated. Now generously add rib rub and continue tossing.

5. Stack meat and vegetables alternating them onto a skewer. This will make a kabob, perfect looking.

6. In the meantime, preheat your Traeger to 500oF with the lid closed for about 15 minutes.

7. Place the kabobs on the grate directly and grill for about 15 minutes.

8. Remove from the Traeger and enjoy it.

Nutrition:

Calories 349,
Total fat 9.7g,
Saturated fat 2.5g,
Total carbs 20.7g,
Net carbs 15.7g,
Protein 46g,
Sugars 13.1g,
Fiber 5g,
Sodium 137mg,
Potassium 1463mg

398. SMOKED SPATCHCOCKED CORNISH GAME HENS

Preparation Time: 25 minutes	Cooking Time: 45 minutes	Servings: 2

Ingredients

4 Cornish game hens

2 oz Traeger big game rub

Directions:

1. Place the hens on a cutting board with breast side down and cut from neck to tailbone with poultry shears. This is to get rid of the backbone and help you see the bird inside.

2. Make a slit in the hen's cartilage at the breastbone base. This is to reveal the keel bone.

3. Now open the bird like a book while holding the ribs with both hands and facing down on your cutting board. Remove keel bone and cut slits behind the bird's legs.

4. Tuck drumsticks into the legs to hold them together.

5. Meanwhile, season the birds on both sides using the rub.

6. Preheat your Traeger to 275oF with the lid closed for about 15 minutes.

7. Now, place the hens with skin side up on the Traeger.

8. Cook for about 45 minutes until the internal temperature reads 160oF.

9. Transfer into a cutting board and rest for about 10 minutes.

10. Serve and enjoy.

Nutrition:

Calories 335,
Total fat 23.5g,
Saturated fat 6.5g,
Total carbs 0g,
Net carbs 0g,
Protein 28.7g,
Sugars 0g,
Fiber 0g,
Sodium 2309mg,
Potassium 316mg

399. SMOKED VENISON TENDERLOIN

Preparation Time: 5 minutes	Cooking Time: 2 hours	Servings: 4

Ingredients

1 lb venison tenderloin

1/4 cup lemon juice

1/4 cup olive oil

5 garlic cloves

1 tbsp salt

1 tbsp black pepper, ground + more for serving

Directions:

1. Place venison tenderloins in a large bowl.

2. Process all the other ingredients in a blender until broken into small pieces and all is incorporated.

3. Pour and massage the marinade over the venison and refrigerate it for about4 hours or overnight.

4. Now remove venison tenderloins from the marinade, rinse, pat dry, and cool at room temperature for about 30 minutes.

5. Preheat your Traeger to 275oF.

6. Place the venison on to your Traeger and smoke for about 2 hours until nice and juicy. Make sure internal temperature reads 130oF to 140oF for rare and medium-rare respectively.

7. Slice and top with more pepper then Remove and rest for about 10 minutes.

Nutrition:

Calories 290,
Total fat 15.5g,
Saturated fat 3.2g,
Total Carbs 2.6g,
Net carbs 2g,
Protein 34.5g,
Sugars 0.4g,
Fiber 0.6g,
Sodium 1813mg,
Potassium 547mg

400. TASTY BBQ RIBS

⏱	🔥	👨‍🍳
Preparation Time: 15 minutes	Cooking Time: 4 hours	Servings: 8

Ingredients

2 ribs racks of ribs

2 1/2 teaspoons brown sugars

1 1/4 teaspoons instant coffees

1 1/4 teaspoons kosher salt

1 1/4 teaspoons garlic powder

1 1/4 teaspoons coriander laces

3/4 teaspoon ground black pepper extra special

1/4 of teaspoon of cocoa powder

1 teaspoon vegetable oil

1 1/2 cups dry red wine

2 tablespoons canola oil

2 tablespoons chopped white onion

2 cups of catsup sauce

1 1/2 cups apple cider vinegar

3/4 cup brown sugar

1 1/2 tablespoons of Maggi chicken broth

3 tablespoons Dijon mustard

2 teaspoons chili powder

2 teaspoons marinated chipotle chili sauce

Nutrition:

Calories: 203,
Fat: 19g,
Carbohydrates: 10g,
Dietary Fiber: 1.3 g,
Protein: 11.1g

Directions:

1. For the ribs: Arrange the racks of ribs on a baking sheet with edges or inside a large roasting pan.

2. Using a knife, remove the membranes from the bone side of the ribs (this step is very important to make the ribs tender).

3. Dry the ribs with a paper towel; Place on the grill with the meat side facing up.

4. Combine the sugar, coffee granules, salt, garlic powder, coriander, pepper and cocoa in the spice grinder; Cover and process until smooth.

5. Lightly rub the ribs with oil.

6. Sprinkle with the mixture, pressing it gently to assist it adhere to the ribs.

7. Let stand at room temperature for not more than 1 hour.

8. Preheat the oven to 250 F. Pour the beer into the bottom of the baking sheet.

9. Cover the bowl with foil, bake for 4 to 5 hours (this will be enough to make the meat tender, but it won't fall off the bones).

10. Prepare the BBQ sauce during the last 30 minutes of baking.

11. Preheat the grill.

12. Grill the ribs over medium heat, turning once, for 5 minutes. Spread with sauce during roasting. Let the ribs stand for 10 minutes before serving.

13. For BBQ sauce: Heat the oil in a medium saucepan over medium heat.

14. Add onion, and then cook for 3 mins or until tender.

15. Add the catsup sauce, vinegar, sugar and broth. Stir until the sugar and the broth dissolve.

16. Add mustard, chili powder and marinade. Cover and cook for 30 minutes. The sauce will thicken as it simmers.

401. GRILLED QUAIL, SOUTH CAROLINA STYLE

Preparation Time: 20 minutes

Cooking Time: 20 minutes

Servings: 4

Ingredients

- **4** tbsp butter
- **1/2** grated onion
- **3-4** tbsp vegetable oil
- **1/2** cup yellow mustard
- **1/2** cup sugar, brown
- **1/2** cup cider vinegar
- **1** tbsp dry mustard
- **1** tbsp cayenne
- **Salt** to taste
- **8-16** quails

Directions:

1. Heat butter over high-medium heat then sauté onions for about 3-4 minutes until translucent.

2. Add all other ingredients except quails and simmer for about 20 minutes. Simmer slowly.

3. Buzz in a blender to make a smooth sauce.

4. Flatten and remove quails backbone by cutting along the side using kitchen shears. Place the quails on a cutting board with breast side up then press them to flatten.

5. Meanwhile, preheat your Traeger to high heat then place then lay your quails with breast side up.

6. Grill the quails with the lid closed for about 5 minutes. Rub the breast side using your sauce as it cooks.

7. Turn over the quails and grill for another 2 minutes with the lid open.

8. Turn over again and rub with sauce once more, cover your Traeger and cook for another 2-4 minutes.

9. Remove quails from the Traeger and rub with sauce once more.

Nutrition:

Calories: 673,
Total fat 40g,
Saturated fat 15g,
Total carbs 31g,
Net carbs 29g,
Protein 45g,
Sugars 28g,
Fiber 2g,
Sodium 579mg,
Potassium 615mg

402. SMOKED MOOSE ROAST WITH CRANBERRY-MINT SAUCE

Preparation Time: 2 hours

Cooking Time: 1 hour 15 minutes

Servings: 6

Ingredients:

- **2-1/2** lbs moose loin roast
- **Salt** to taste, kosher
- **2** tbsp olive oil
- **Favorite** rub
- **1** can, 14-oz, cranberry sauce, whole berry
- **1/4** tbsp cardamom, ground
- **1** tbsp chopped mint, fresh and packed
- **Cracked** pepper to taste, fresh

Directions:

1. Tie moose roast using kitchen wire and season with salt then let it sit for 2 hours at room temperature. Once 2 hours are over, pat dry using paper towels.

2. Preheat a Traeger to 275oF.

3. Meanwhile, heat oil over high-medium heat in a pan until oil starts to smoke. Now sear your meat until a golden crust on all sides.

4. Remove meat from the pan and splash with rub generously.

5. Smoke the meat in your Traeger for about 1 hour until internal temperature reads 125oF.

6. Remove meat and loosely wrap in foil then allow your meat to carry over until 135oF for medium-rare.

7. In the meantime, combine cranberry sauce, cardamom, mint, pepper, and salt. Heat on low occasionally stirring until warmed through.

8. Once the meat has rested for about 10-15 minutes, slice the meat against the grain.

9. Serve with cranberry-mint sauce.

10. Enjoy with sides of choice.

Nutrition:

Calories 1141,
Total fat 12.4g,
Saturated fat 3g,
Total carbs 6.3g,
Net carbs 3.7g,
Protein 232.4g,
Sugars 2.4g,
Fiber 2.6g,
Sodium 575mg,
Potassium 2771mg

403. SMOKED GUINEA FOWL WITH CRANBERRY/ORANGE GLAZE

Preparation Time: 25 minutes

Cooking Time: 1 hour 45 minutes

Servings: 8

Ingredients

1 guinea fowl

For the rub

3 tbsp salt

1 tbsp pepper

2 tbsp ginger powder

2 tbsp cinnamon powder

2 tbsp oregano, dried

Cranberry-orange glaze

2 cups chicken broth

1 orange juice

2/3 cup cranberry jam

A pinch of cinnamon powder

A pinch of ginger powder

Directions:

1. Mix all the sauce ingredients in a medium saucepan and boil.

2. Lower heat and cook gently until sauce reduces having a syrup texture.

3. Meanwhile, mix all rub ingredients using your hands breaking up any clumps.

4. Search a hole on the guinea fowl neck. This is to slice your finger underneath the guinea fowl skin. Now separate meat from the skin and apply rub between the skin and the meat.

5. Poke holes with a sharp knife in the sin and rub its abdominal cavity.

6. Refrigerate the guinea fowl for a few hours.

7. In the meantime, preheat your Traeger to 250oF.

8. Smoke your guinea fowl until internal temperature reads 50oC.

9. Turn heat to 845oF then splash guinea fowl with sunflower oil. This is to crisp skin.

10. Bake until golden brown tint on the skin and internal temperature reads 65oC.

11. Apply a thin glaze layer on the guinea fowl just a few minutes before internal temperate is reached.

12. Grill until glaze sticks on the skins and slightly caramelize the skin.

Nutrition:

Calories 539,

Total fat 8.8g,

Saturated fat 2.5g,

Total carbs 29.6g,

Net carbs 28.4g,

Protein 79g,

Sugars 22.9g,

Fiber 1.2g,

Sodium 3911mg,

Potassium 656mg

404. SMOKED DOVES

 Preparation
Time: 30 minutes

 Cooking Time:
2 hours

 Servings:
10

Ingredients:

1/2 cup kosher salt

2 quarts water

16-20 doves

Optional: 1 tbsp instacure no.1

For guajillo sauce

5 unpeeled garlic cloves

1 quartered white onion, small and roughly chopped

2-5 hot chiles

8 guajillo peppers, dried and stems/seeds removed

2 tbsp tomato paste

1 tbsp Mexican oregano, dried

1/4 tbsp allspice

1/4 tbsp coriander, ground

Salt to taste

Lime juice to taste

Directions:

1. Dissolve salt in water then submerge the doves in the water. Refrigerate for about 4 hours. Now remove from the fridge, rinse and pat them dry.

2. Preheat your Traeger to 170oF-200oF.

3. Place the doves on the Traeger and smoke for about 2 hours.

4. In the meantime, rehydrate chiles by pouring boiling water over.

5. Char garlic and onions in a dry skillet, hot, until nice blackening. Now peel the garlic and place both onions and garlic in a blender.

6. Add chiles and remaining sauce ingredients into your blender. Process until smooth while adjusting seasoning with lime juice and salt. You can add water to thin the sauce.

7. Remove the doves from the Traeger, half them using kitchen shears and coat with the sauce.

8. Serve and enjoy with napkins and bone bowl.

Nutrition:

Calories 610,
Total fat 19.7g,
Saturated fat 0g,
Total carbs 3.6g,
Net carbs 3g,
Protein 101.2g,
Sugars 1.4g,
Fiber 0.6g,
Sodium 5728mg,
Potassium 68mg

405. SOY MARINADE SWEET SMOKED VENISON BRISKET

Preparation Time: 25 minutes

Cooking Time: 6 hours

Servings: 10

Ingredients

Venison brisket (6-lb., 2.7-kg.)

The Marinade

Olive oil - ½ cup

Balsamic vinegar - ½ cup

Worcestershire sauce - ½ cup

Soy sauce - ½ cup

Dijon mustard - 1 tablespoon

Minced garlic - 2 tablespoons

Kosher salt - 1 ½ teaspoon

Pepper - 2 teaspoons

The Rub

Salt - 1 teaspoon

Brown sugar - ½ cup

Garlic powder - 2 tablespoons

Ground black pepper - 1 tablespoon

Smoked paprika - 2 tablespoons

Cumin - 1 tablespoon

The Heat

Hickory wood pellets

Directions:

1. Combine olive oil with balsamic vinegar, Worcestershire sauce, and soy sauce in a container. Mix well.

2. Season the liquid mixture with Dijon mustard, minced garlic, salt, and pepper then stir until incorporated.

3. Add the venison brisket to the liquid mixture and marinate it for at least 4 hours or overnight. Store the marinated venison brisket in the refrigerator to keep it fresh.

4. On the next day, take the marinated venison brisket out of the refrigerator and thaw it at room temperature.

5. In the meantime, combine the rub ingredients--salt, brown sugar, garlic powder, ground black pepper, smoked paprika, and cumin. Mix well.

6. Sprinkle the rub ingredients over the venison brisket then set aside.

7. Plug the wood pellet smoker and place the wood pellet inside the hopper. Turn the switch on.

8. Set the temperature to 250ºF (121ºC) and prepare the wood pellet smoker for indirect heat. Wait until the wood pellet smoker is ready.

9. Insert the seasoned venison brisket into the preheated wood pellet smoker and smoke it for 6 hours.

10. Regularly check the internal temperature of the smoked venison brisket and once it reaches 140ºF (60ºC), remove it from the wood pellet smoker.

11. Transfer the smoked venison brisket to a serving dish and serve.

Nutrition:

Calories: 257,

Fat: 10g,

Carbohydrates: 10g,

Dietary Fiber: 1.3 g,

Protein: 11.1g

406. GRILLED ULTIMATE GAME BURGER

Preparation Time: 10 minutes	Cooking Time: 15 minutes	Servings: 2

Ingredients

3/4 lb. wild boar, ground

3/4 lb. venison, ground

Pepper to taste

Salt to taste

2 tbsp. mayonnaise

1 tbsp. ketchup

2 tbsp. sweet pickle relish

1/2 tbsp. sugar

1/2 tbsp. white vinegar

1 sliced white onion

4 buns

4 American cheese pieces

4 lettuce pieces

1 sliced tomato

1. Place and combine venison and boar in a bowl, mixing. Do not overwork.

Directions:

2. Form 4, 1/3 lb. patties, from the meat mixture and generously splash with pepper and salt.

3. Mix all sauce ingredients in a bowl and set aside.

4. Start your Traeger on smoke for about 4-5 minutes with the lid open until fire establishes.

5. Preheat the Traeger to 400oF while lid closed for about 10-15 minutes.

6. Now arrange the patties on the Traeger grill grate.

7. Cook until the desired doneness and until internal temperature reaches 160oF. Flip once.

8. Place the sliced onion on the grill 5 minutes before cooking is over.

9. During the last minutes, place cheese on your burgers and your buns on the grill.

10. Remove and build the burgers with a burger patty, bun, lettuce, tomato, and the grilled onions.

Nutrition:

Calories 256,

Total fat 6g,

Saturated fat 1.1g,

Total carbs 9.4g,

Net carbs 8.7g,

Protein 37.2g,

Sugars 6.2g,

Fiber 0.7g,

Sodium 195mg,

Potassium 59mg

407. WILD BOAR

Preparation Time: 20 minutes	Cooking Time: 6 hours	Servings: 4

Ingredients:

1 (4 pounds) wild boar roast

2 cups BBQ sauce

Marinade:

1 tbsp chopped fresh thyme

1/3 cup honey

One-fourth cup soy sauce

One-fourth tsp cayenne pepper

One-half tsp oregano

One-fourth cup balsamic vinegar

One-half tsp garlic powder

1 cup apple juice

Directions:

1. Roast the wild boar at 350 F for approximately 20 minutes or until internal temperature reaches 145 degrees Fahrenheit.

2. While the meat is cooking, combine all ingredients for the marinade in a bowl.

3. Marinate the meat for 6 hours in the refrigerator.

4. Drain the meat from the marinade.

5. Pour the marinade over the roast, cover, and cook on low for 5-6 hours

6. Serve with roasted potatoes.

Nutrition:

Energy (calories): 214 kcal

Protein: 3.49 g

Fat: 3.23 g

Carbohydrates: 46.07 g

408. GOAT CHOPS

 Preparation Time: 5 minutes

 Cooking Time: 8 minutes

 Servings: 8

Ingredients:

8 1-inch thick goat chops

Marinade:

6 garlic cloves (minced)

1 tbsp dried oregano

One-fourth tsp salt

1 tsp ground black pepper

One-half cup dry white wine

1 lemon (juiced)

1 tbsp grated lemon zest

1 onion (chopped)

Directions:

1. Combine all the marinade ingredients in a mixing bowl. Add the goat chops and toss to combine. Leave the goat chops in the marinade for about 30 minutes.

2. Start the grill on smoke mode, leaving the lid opened for 5 minutes for fire to start.

3. Close the lid and preheat the grill to HIGH, with lid closed for 15 minutes.

4. Place the goat chops on the grill grate and smoke for 8 minutes, 4 minutes per side.

5. Remove goat chops from heat and let it cool for a few minutes.

6. Serve.

Nutrition:

Energy (calories): 1121 kcal

Protein: 207.85 g

Fat: 24.63 g

Carbohydrates: 2.93 g

409. SMOKED GOOSE BREAST

 Preparation Time: 15 minutes

Cooking Time: 45 minutes

 Servings: 8

Ingredients:

8 goose breasts

Marinade:

4 tbsp soy sauce

5 tbsp brown sugar

4 tbsp honey

1 tsp garlic powder

1 tbsp Dijon mustard

1/3 cup olive oil

One-half cup pineapple juice

1 tsp paprika

One-half tsp cayenne pepper

Directions:

1. Mix together soy sauce, brown sugar, honey, garlic powder and mustard.

2. Place goose breasts in a baking dish. Pour marinade over goose, reserving 2 tbsp of marinade for sauce.

3. marinade for sauce. Reserve 1/3 of the marinade for sauce.

4. Marinate the goose breasts for 15 minutes.

5. Set aside pineapple juice. Mix with rest of marinade and paprika.

6. Heat the Traeger grill smoker.

7. Place breasts skin down in Smoker for 45 minutes.

8. Pour marinade over goose breasts. Cover pan, and reduce heat to medium-low. Cook for 40 minutes. Rest for 5 minutes, then slice thinly. Drizzle with reserved sauce and pineapple juice.

Nutrition:

Energy (calories): 2633 kcal

Protein: 349.39 g

Fat: 119.72 g

Carbohydrates: 18.68 g

410. CHILI COFFEE SMOKED CORNISH

🕐	🔥	👨‍🍳
Preparation Time: 25 minutes	Cooking Time: 2 hours 10 minutes	Servings: 2

Ingredients

Cornish (5-lb., 2.3-kg.)

The Brine

Brewed coffee - 4 cups

Water - 2 cups

Kosher salt - 3 tablespoons

Minced garlic - 1 tablespoon

Chopped red onion - 2 tablespoons

Chili powder - 2 teaspoons

Bay leaves - 2

The Rub

Ground coffee - 2 tablespoons

Smoked paprika - 2 teaspoons

Dry oregano - 2 tablespoons

Brown sugar - ½ cup

Dried mustard - 1 teaspoon

Chili powder - 1 ½ teaspoon

Cayenne pepper - ½ teaspoon

Balsamic vinegar - 2 tablespoons

The Heat

Hickory wood pellets

Directions:

1. Pour brewed coffee together with water into a container then season the mixture with salt, minced garlic, chopped red onion, chili powder, and bay leaves. Stir well.

2. Put the Cornish into the brine mixture and soak it for at least 6 hours or overnight. Store it in the refrigerator to keep the Cornish fresh.

3. On the next day, remove the Cornish from the refrigerator and take it out of the brine.

4. Wash and rinse the Cornish and pat it dry. Set aside.

5. Next, combine the rub ingredients--ground coffee, smoked paprika, dry oregano, brown sugar, dried mustard, chili powder, cayenne pepper, and balsamic vinegar then rub it over the Cornish.

6. Plug the wood pellet smoker and place the wood pellet inside the hopper. Turn the switch on.

7. Set the temperature to 250°F (121°C) and prepare the wood pellet smoker for indirect heat. Wait until the wood pellet smoker is ready.

8. Place the Cornish in the wood pellet smoker and smoke it for 2 hours.

9. Check the internal temperature of the smoked Cornish and once it reaches 165°F (74°C), remove it from the wood pellet smoker.

10. Transfer the smoked Cornish to a serving dish and serve.

Nutrition:

Calories: 187,

Fat: 18g,

Carbohydrates: 23g,

Dietary Fiber: 1.3 g,

Protein: 16.1g

411. WHITE WINE SMOKED RABBIT GARLIC

Preparation Time: 15 minutes	Cooking Time: 2 hours 10 minutes	Servings: 5

Ingredients

Rabbit (6-lb., 2.7-kg.)

The Marinade

Olive oil - 1 cup

Red wine vinegar - 2 tablespoons

Minced garlic - ¼ cup

Kosher salt - 2 tablespoons

Pepper - 1 ½ teaspoon

Bay leaves - 2

Fresh rosemary leaves - 2 sprigs

Lemon juice - 3 tablespoons

White wine - ¼ cup

The Heat

Apple wood pellets

Directions:

1. Combine the entire marinade ingredients--olive oil, red wine vinegar, minced garlic, kosher salt, pepper, bay leaves, fresh rosemary, lemon juice, and white wine. Mix well.

2. Rub the spice mixture over the rabbit and place it in a disposable aluminum pan.

3. Cover the rabbit with plastic wrap then marinate it for at least 2 hours. Store the rabbit in the refrigerator to keep it fresh.

4. After 2 hours, take the rabbit out of the refrigerator and thaw it at room temperature.

5. Plug the wood pellet smoker and place the wood pellet inside the hopper. Turn the switch on.

6. Set the temperature to 275°F (135°C) and prepare the wood pellet smoker for indirect heat. Wait until the wood pellet smoker is ready.

7. Insert the aluminum pan with the rabbit into the wood pellet smoker and smoke it for 2 hours.

8. Once the internal temperature of the smoked rabbit reaches 165°F (74°C), remove it from the wood pellet smoker and transfer it to a serving dish.

Nutrition:

Calories: 157,

Fat: 10g,

Carbohydrates: 10g,

Dietary Fiber: 1.3 g,

Protein: 11.1g

412. SMOKED RABBIT

Preparation Time: 15 minutes	Cooking Time: 3 hours	Servings: 4

Ingredients:

1 (3 pounds) whole rabbit

1 tbsp dried rosemary

1/3 cup olive oil

1 tbsp dried thyme

1 tbsp cracked black pepper

1 tsp sea salt

One-half cup dry white wine

1 cup apple juice

1 tbsp dried oregano

1 tbsp freshly grated lemon zest

Directions:

1. Rinse and pat dry the rabbit. Cover it with the dried rosemary, olive oil, thyme, black pepper and sea salt, making sure the entire rabbit is coated.

2. Cover the rabbit with plastic wrap and place it in the refrigerator.

3. Consume within two to three days. Thaw overnight and refrigerate for 8 hours. Season the rabbit with the white wine, apple juice, oregano and lemon zest.

4. Cover with a layer of plastic wrap and refrigerate overnight. Heat up your barbecue/smoking machine to medium heat. Place the rabbit on the smoker. Smoke it for three hours, or until the liquid in the pan reduces by three quarters.

5. Check every hour to baste the rabbit with the reduced liquid. When finished, remove from smoker and let the rabbit cool down. Slice to serve.

Nutrition:

Energy (calories): 232 kcal

Protein: 3.27 g

Fat: 20.96 g

Carbohydrates: 8.86 g

413. SPATCHCOCK SMOKED QUAIL

Preparation Time: 15 minutes	Cooking Time: 1 hours	Servings: 4

Ingredients:

4 quails

2 tbsp finely chopped fresh parsley

1 tbsp finely chopped fresh rosemary

2 tbsp finely chopped fresh thyme

One-half cup melted butter

1 tsp garlic powder

1 tsp onion powder

1 tsp ground black pepper

2 tsp salt or to taste

2 tbsp finely chopped scallions

Directions:

1. Remove the giblets from the quail; set aside. Rinse the quails under cold running water, and pat dry with paper towels. Prepare the grill for cooking; place the quail on the grill rack, and brush them with butter. Cook about 1 hour, brushing with melted butter every 5 minutes, until evenly brown.

2. The internal temperature should reach 170 deg. F. Meanwhile, prepare a marinade by combining the fresh herbs, scallions, garlic, onion powders, salt, ground black pepper and salt; mix well.

3. Prepare the quail; pour the marinade over the quail, and place them in a glass baking dish, seam-side down. Cover with plastic wrap, and refrigerate overnight.

4. Serve with mashed potatoes and roasted vegetables.

Nutrition:

Energy (calories): 337 kcal

Protein: 20.72 g

Fat: 27.28 g

Carbohydrates: 2.24 g

414. SMOKED PHEASANT

| Preparation Time: 15 minu-tes | Cooking Time: 5 hours | Servings: 5 |

Ingredients:

2 whole pheasants

4 tbsp brown sugar

1 tbsp kosher salt

1 tbsp black peppercorns

4 cups water

2 cups maple syrup

1 cup pineapple juice

1 tbsp Dijon mustard

Directions:

1. Rinse pheasant, pat dry. Rub all over with brown sugar, salt & pepper.

2. Place 4 cups water in the bottom of a pot with high sides. Place pheasants in pot, bring to a boil for 20-30 minutes. Turn off the heat, drain off liquid through a strainer. Pat dry.

3. Place breast-side up on a rack inside a roasting pan, with the rack sitting in low boiling water. Spoon on maple syrup, pineapple juice & mustard.

4. Cover with foil. Roast for 4 hours at 250°F, basting regularly with the juices in the pan. Remove foil and roast for 4 hours more, basting whenever possible. Enjoy!

Nutrition:

Energy (calories): 767 kcal

Protein: 67.27 g

Fat: 10.5 g

Carbohydrates: 100.37 g

415. RABBIT STEW

| Preparation Time: 15 minutes | Cooking Time: 2 h + 30 minutes | Servings: 4 |

Ingredients:

1 (3 pounds) rabbit (cut into bite sizes)

One-fourth cup olive oil

1 medium onion (chopped)

1 carrot (diced)

1 stalk celery (diced)

2 roman tomato (sliced)

1 red bell pepper (sliced)

2 garlic cloves (minced)

1 cup red wine

4 cups chicken broth

2 bay leaves

2 tbsp flour

1 tsp dried thyme

1 tsp salt

1 tsp ground black pepper

Directions:

1. Prepare your grilling machine.

2. In a large pot over medium heat, add in olive oil and heat. Sauté onion, celery, carrot, red bell pepper, and garlic for 2 minutes, stirring constantly.

3. Add in rabbit pieces, red wine, dried thyme, bay leaves, salt, & ground black pepper. Stir to coat rabbit. Add in enough broth so that rabbit is submerged, then cover.

4. Bring to a boil then turn heat to low. Simmer for at least 2 hours. Check occasionally to make sure rabbit is submerged and that there is adequate liquid.

5. Mix together 4 tbsp flour and 1 cup of broth. Slowly stir into rabbit. Continue cooking on low heat uncovered for 30 minutes until rabbit is tender.

Nutrition:

Energy (calories): 554 kcal

Protein: 53.96 g

Fat: 30.42 g

Carbohydrates: 14.01 g

416. GRILLED ANTELOPE

Preparation Time: 10 minutes and overnight	Cooking Time: 15 minutes	Servings: 8

Ingredients:

1-pound antelope steak (slices into 1-inch thick slices)

Marinade:

4 tbsp olive oil

One-half tsp dried rosemary

2 garlic cloves (minced)

1 lemon (juice)

One-fourth cup balsamic vinegar

One-half tsp salt or to taste

1 tsp onion powder

One-fourth tsp thyme

1 tsp oregano

1 tsp paprika

Directions:

1. Place all the ingredients in a zip lock bag and toss to coat the meat. Seal tightly and refrigerate for at least 1 hour or overnight.

2. Preheat a grill on medium-high heat, brush the grill with some oil. Remove the meat from the marinade and place it on the grill. Close the lid and cook until the meat is well grilled on both sides and is tender when pierced with a fork. Serve hot.

Nutrition:

Energy (calories): 186 kcal

Protein: 15.97 g

Fat: 12.57 g

Carbohydrates: 2.52 g

417. ELK KEBABS

P

Peparation Time: 10 minutes	Cooking Time: 12 minutes	Servings: 4

Ingredients:

2 elk steaks (cut into 2-inch cubes)

1 large bell pepper (sliced)

1 large yellow bell pepper (sliced)

1 large green bell pepper (sliced)

1 onion (sliced)

10 medium cremini mushrooms (destemmed and halved)

Wooden or bamboo skewers (soaked in water for 30 minutes, at least)

Marinade:

1 tbsp soy sauce

1 tsp garlic powder

One-half tsp ground black pepper

1 tbsp Worcestershire sauce

1 tbsp lemon juice

1 tsp onion powder

3 tbsp olive oil

1 tsp paprika

1. In a large mixing bowl, combine all the

Directions:

marinade ingredients. Add the elk and mushroom. Toss to combine. Cover the bowl tightly with aluminum foil and refrigerate for 8 hours.

2. Remove the mushroom and elk from the marinade.

3. Thread the bell peppers, onion, mushroom and elk onto skewers to make kabobs.

4. Preheat your grill to HIGH with lid closed for 15 minutes, using mesquite hardwood pellets.

5. Arrange the kebobs onto the grill grate and grill for 12 minutes, 6 minutes per side, or until the internal temperature of the elk reaches 145°F.

6. Remove kebabs from heat. Serve warm and enjoy.

Nutrition:

Energy (calories): 148 kcal

Protein: 3.05 g

Fat: 11.2 g

Carbohydrates: 11.19 g

418. SMOKED GOOSE BREAST TERIYAKI

	🔥	👨‍🍳
Preparation Time: 25 minutes	Cooking Time: 2 hours 10 minutes	Servings: 2

Ingredients

Goose breast (4-lbs., 1.8-kg.)

The Marinade

Teriyaki sauce - ½ cup

Soy sauce - ¼ cup

Sherry wine - ¼ cup

Olive oil - 1.2 cup

Chopped onion - ¼ cup

Minced garlic - 2 tablespoons

Ginger powder - 1 teaspoon

Kosher salt - 1 teaspoon

Pepper - ½ teaspoon

The Heat

Cherry wood pellets

Directions:

1. Mix the teriyaki sauce with soy sauce, sherry wine, and olive oil. Stir until incorporated.

2. Add chopped onion, minced garlic, ginger powder, kosher salt, and pepper to the liquid mixture then mix well.

3. Score the goose breast at several places then put it into the liquid mixture.

4. Marinate the goose breast for approximately 2 hours and store it in the refrigerator to keep the goose fresh.

5. After 2 hours, take the goose breast out of the refrigerator and thaw it at room temperature.

6. Plug the wood pellet smoker and place the wood pellet inside the hopper. Turn the switch on.

7. Set the temperature to 275°F (135°C) and prepare the wood pellet smoker for indirect heat. Wait until the wood pellet smoker is ready.

8. Arrange the marinated goose breast in the wood pellet smoker and smoke it for 2 hours.

9. Baste the remaining marinade mixture and repeat it once every 30 minutes.

10. Once the internal temperature of the smoked goose breast reaches 170°F (77°C), remove it from the wood pellet smoker.

Nutrition:

Calories: 203,

Fat: 12g,

Carbohydrates: 18g,

Dietary Fiber: 1.3 g,

Protein: 14.1g

Chapter 4.

COLD SMOKING

419. SMOKED VEGGIE MEDLEY

| Preparation Time: 30 minutes | Cooking Time: 60 minutes | Servings: 4 |

Ingredients:

1 Spanish red onion, peeled and cut into quarters

1 red pepper, seeded and sliced

2 zucchinis, sliced

1 yellow summer squash, sliced

Olive oil – 2 tablespoons

Balsamic vinegar – 2 tablespoons

6 garlic cloves, peeled, minced

Sea salt – 1 teaspoon

Black pepper – ½ teaspoon

Directions:

1. Preheat the pellet grill to 350°F.

2. In a large bowl, combine the red onion, red pepper, zucchinis, summer squash, olive oil, balsamic vinegar, garlic, sea salt, and black pepper. Toss to combine.

3. Transfer the veggies to the smoker and with the lid closed cook for between 30-45 minutes, until cooked through and caramelized.

4. Serve and enjoy.

Nutrition:

Calories: 63

Protein: 3g

Carbs: 9g

Fat: 3g

420. FETA CHEESE STUFFED MEATBALLS

| Preparation Time: 30 minutes | Cooking Time: 35 minutes | Servings: 6 |

Ingredients:

Pepper

Salt

¾ c. Feta cheese

½ t. thyme

Two t. chopped oregano

Zest of one lemon

One pound ground pork

One pound ground beef

One T. olive oil

Directions:

1. Place the pepper, salt, thyme, oregano, olive oil, lemon zest, and ground meats into a large bowl.

2. Combine thoroughly the ingredients using your hands.

3. Cut the Feta into little cubes and begin making the meatballs. Take a half tablespoon of the meat mixture and roll it around a piece of cheese. Continue until all meat has been used.

4. Add wood pellets to your smoker and follow your cooker's startup procedure. Preheat your smoker, with your lid closed, until it reaches 350.

5. Brush the meatballs with more olive oil and put onto the grill. Grill for ten minutes until browned.

Nutrition:

Calories: 294.5

Protein: 28.4g

Carbs: 15.2g

Fat: 12.8g

421. MEDITERRANEAN MEATBALLS

Preparation Time: 30 minutes	Cooking Time: 40 minutes	Servings: 6

Ingredients:

Pepper

Salt

One t. vinegar

Two T. olive oil

Two eggs

One chopped onion

One soaked slice of bread

½ t. cumin

One T. chopped basil

1 ½ T. chopped parsley

2 ½ pounds ground beef

Directions:

1. Use your hands to combine everything together until thoroughly combined. If needed, when forming meatballs, dip your hands into some water. Shape into 12 meatballs.

2. Add wood pellets to your smoker and follow your cooker's startup procedure. Preheat your smoker, with your lid closed, until it reaches 380.

3. Place the meatballs onto the grill and cook on all sides for eight minutes. Switch off the heat then let rest for five minutes.

4. Serve with favorite condiments or a salad.

Nutrition:

Calories: 403

Protein: 24.5g

Carbs: 31.5g

Fat: 17.5g

422. BUTTERNUT SQUASH

Preparation Time: 30 minutes	Cooking Time: 2hours	Servings: 4

Ingredients:

Brown sugar

Maple syrup

6 T. butter

Butternut squash

Directions:

1. Add wood pellets to your smoker and follow your cooker's startup procedure. Preheat your smoke, with your lid closed, until it reaches 300.

2. Slice the squash in half, lengthwise. Clean out all the seeds and membrane.

3. Place this cut-side down on the grill and smoke for 30 minutes. Flip the squash over and cook for another 30 minutes.

4. Place each half of the squash onto aluminum foil. Sprinkle each half with brown sugar and maple syrup, and put 3 T. of butter onto each. Wrap foil around to create a tight seal.

5. Increase temperature to 400 and place onto the grill for another 35 minutes.

6. Carefully unwrap each half making sure to reserve juices in the bottom. Place onto serving platter and drizzle juices over each half. Use a spoon to scoop out and enjoy.

Nutrition:

Calories: 82

Protein: 1.8g

Carbs: 21.5g

Fat: 0.18g

423. CAJUN ARTICHOKES

Preparation Time: 30 minutes	Cooking Time: 2 hours	Servings: 4

Ingredients:

1 2-16 canned, whole artichoke hearts

Cajun seasoning – 2 tablespoons

Hickory wood pellets

Directions:

1. Preheat the smoker, for cold smoking

2. Slice the artichoke hearts in half.

3. Toss the artichoke halves in the Cajun seasoning.

4. Spread the hearts in a single layer on the smoker rack and cold smoke for 2 hours.

5. Serve and enjoy.

Nutrition:

Calories: 25
Protein: 3g
Carbs: 9g   Fat: 0g

---

424. FOR MAGGI MACARONI AND CHEESE

Preparation Time: 30 minutes	Cooking Time: 1 hour 30 minutes	Servings: 8

Ingredients:

¼ c. all-purpose flour

½ stick butter

Butter, for greasing

One pound cooked elbow macaroni

One c. grated Parmesan

8 ounces cream cheese

Two c. shredded Monterey Jack

3 t. garlic powder

Two t. salt

One t. pepper

Two c. shredded Cheddar, divided

3 c. milk

Directions:

1. Put the butter into the pot and melt. Mix in the flour. Stir constantly for a minute. Mix in the pepper, salt, garlic powder, and milk. Let it boil.

2. After lowering the heat, let it simmer for about 5 mins, or until it has thickened. Remove from the heat.

3. Mix in the cream cheese, parmesan, Monterey jack, and 1 ½ c. of cheddar. Stir everything until melted. Fold in the pasta.

4. Add wood pellets to your smoker and follow your cooker's startup procedure. Preheat your smoker, with your lid closed, until it reaches 225.

5. Butter a 9" x 13" baking pan. Pour the macaroni mixture to the pan and lay on the grill. Cover and allow it to smoke for an hour, or until it has become bubbly. Top the macaroni with rest of the cheddar during the last

6. Serve.

Nutrition:

Calories: 493
Protein: 19.29g
Carbs: 52.15g
Fat: 22.84g

425. SMOKED OLIVES

Preparation Time: 30 minutes	Cooking Time: 1 hour 15 minutes	Servings: 4

Ingredients:

Kalamata olives, pitted, drained – 1 cup

Green olives, drained – 1 cup

Extra-virgin olive oil – 2 tablespoons

White wine – 2 tablespoons

2 cloves of garlic, peeled, and minced

Dried rosemary – ¾ teaspoon

Freshly ground black pepper

Asiago cheese, freshly grated, to serve, optional

Directions:

1. Preheat the pellet grill to 220°F

2. Arrange the olives on a sheet of heavy aluminum foil molded into a small foil tray.

3. Add the olive oil, white wine, garlic, dried rosemary, and black pepper. Toss to coat evenly.

4. Transfer the olives to the smoker and cook for between 30-50 minutes, until smoky in flavor. It is recommended to check the smoking process after 20 minutes.

5. Serve with the grated cheese and enjoy.

Nutrition:

Calories: 40
Protein: 0g
Carbs: 1g   Fat: 4g

426. GREEK MEATBALLS

Preparation Time: 30 minutes	Cooking Time: 35 minutes	Servings: 8

Ingredients:

Pepper

Salt

One t. thyme

One t. cumin

One T. oregano

Two T. chopped parsley

¼ c. olive oil

Two chopped green onions

One T. almond flour

Two eggs

½ pound ground pork

2 ½ pound ground beef

Directions:

1. Mix all the ingredients together using your hands until everything is incorporated evenly. Form mixture into meatballs until all meat is used.

2. Add wood pellets to your smoker and follow your cooker's startup procedure. Preheat your smoker, with your lid closed, until it reaches 380.

3. Brush the meatballs with olive oil and place onto grill. Cook for ten minutes on all sides.

Nutrition:

Calories: 337
Protein: 33g
Carbs: 12g   Fat: 16g

427. SUMMER TREAT CORN

 Preparation time: 10 minutes

 Cooking time: 20 minutes

Servings: 6

Ingredients
6 fresh whole corn on the cob

One-half C. butter

Salt

Directions:
1. Set the temperature of Traeger Grill to 400 degrees F and preheat with closed lid for 15 mins.

2. Husk the corn and remove all the silk.

3. Brush each corn with melted butter and sprinkle with salt.

4. Place the corn onto the grill and cook for about 20 mins, rotating after every 5 mins and brushing with butter once halfway through.

5. Serve warm.

Nutrition:
Calories 334;
Carbohydrates: 43.5g;
Protein: 7.7g

428. SPICY BARBECUE PECANS

 Preparation Time: 30 minutes

 Cooking Time: 1 hour

 Servings: 6

Ingredients:
2 ½ t. garlic powder

16 ounces raw pecan halves

One t. onion powder

One t. pepper

Two t. salt

One t. dried thyme

Butter, for greasing

3 T. melted butter

Directions:
1. Add wood pellets to your smoker and follow your cooker's startup procedure. Preheat your smoker, with your lid closed, until it reaches 225.

2. Place parchment on a baking sheet and coat with some butter.

3. Mix the thyme, salt, onion powder, pepper, garlic powder, and butter together. Add in the pecans and toss everything to coat.

4. Pour the nuts onto the baking pan and place them on the grill.

5. Cover and smoke for an hour, flipping the nuts one. Make sure the nuts are toasted and heated. They should be removed from the grill. Set aside to cool and dry.

6. These can be kept for three weeks in an airtight container.

Nutrition:
Calories: 188
Protein: 2.5g
Carbs: 3.78g
Fat: 19.61g

429. CRUNCHY POTATO WEDGES

Preparation time: 15 minutes	Cooking time 16minutes	Servings: 5

Ingredients

4 Yukon gold potatoes

2 tbsp. olive oil

1 tbsp. garlic, minced

2 tsp. onion powder

One-half tsp. red pepper flakes, crushed

Salt and freshly ground black pepper, to taste

Directions:

1. Keep the oven of the Traeger Grill to 400 degrees F and heat it up it for 15 minutes with the cover closed.

2. Cut each potato into 8 equal-sized wedges.

3. In a large bowl, add potato wedges and remaining ingredients and toss to coat well.

4. Arrange the potato wedges onto the grill and cook for about 8 mins per side.

5. Remove from grill and serve hot.

Nutrition:

Calories: 157;

Carbohydrates: 25.7g;

Protein: 3g;

430. TWICE GRILLED POTATOES

Preparation time: 20 minutes	Cooking time 4 hours	Servings: 4

Ingredients

6 russet potatoes

2 tbsp. olive oil

Salt

8 cooked bacon slices, crumbled

One-half C. heavy whipping cream

4 oz. cream cheese, softened

4 tbsp. butter, softened

1 tsp. seasoned salt

2 C. Monterrey Jack cheese, grated and divided

Directions:

1. Preheat oven to 500 degrees.

2. Cut potatoes into thin wedges and transfer to a large bowl.

3. Add 1 Tbsp. oil, and salt, to bowl. Toss to coat.

4. Separate potatoes into 2 even piles on baking sheet.

5. Bake 4 hours, turning once. Remove from oven and let cool.

6. Turn oven to broil. Combine cream, butter, and 2 tbsp. of cheese.

7. Place potatoes into 2 10-oz. or 1 6-oz. oven-save bowl.

8. Top with half of the cheese, then half of the cream mixture.

9. Repeat layers. Broil until cream cheese is bubbly and golden.

10. Top with remaining 2 tbsp. olive oil and seasoned salt.

11. Serve.

Nutrition:

Calories 539;

Carbohydrates: 35.7g;

Protein: 17.6g

431. MOUTHWATERING CAULIFLOWER

| Preparation time: 15 minutes | Cooking time: 30 minutes | Servings: 8 |

Ingredients

2 large heads cauliflower head, stem removed and cut into 2-inch florets

3 tbsp. olive oil

Salt

ground black pepper

One-fourth C parsley, chopped finely

Directions:

1. Control the frequency of the grill to 500 degrees F and set the temperature this for 15 minutes with the lid close.

2. Add cauliflower florets, oil, salt and black pepper and toss to coat well.

3. Divide the cauliflower florets onto 2 baking sheets and spread in an even layer.

4. Place the baking sheets onto the grill and cook for about 20-30 mins, stirring once after 15 mins.

5. Transfer into a large bowl.

6. Add the parsley and toss to coat well.

7. Serve.

Nutrition:

Calories 62;
Carbohydrates: 3.6g;
Protein: 1.4g

432. SUPER-ADDICTING MUSHROOMS

| Preparation time: 15 minutes | Cooking time 45 minutes | Servings: 4 |

Ingredients

4 C. fresh whole baby Portobello mushrooms, cleaned

1 tbsp. canola oil

1 tsp. granulated garlic

1 tsp. onion powder

Salt and freshly ground black pepper, to taste

Directions:

1. Put a Traeger Grill fire to 180 degrees F and pre - heat for 15 mins with the cover closed, using charcoal.

2. Add all ingredients and mix well.

3. Place the mushrooms onto the grill and cook for about 30 mins.

4. Preheat the Grill to 400 degrees F and preheat with closed lid for 15 mins.

5. Place the mushrooms onto the grill and cook for about 15 mins.

6. Serve warm.

Nutrition:

Calories 50;
Carbohydrates: 3.3g;
Protein: 2.4g

433. VEGGIE LOVER'S BURGERS

| Preparation time: 20 minutes | Cooking time 47 minutes | Servings: 6 |

Ingredients

Three-fourth C. lentils

1 tbsp. ground flaxseed

2 tbsp. extra-virgin olive oil

1 onion, chopped

2 garlic cloves, minced

Salt

black pepper

1 C. walnuts, toasted

Three-fourth C. breadcrumbs

1 tsp. ground cumin

1 tsp. paprika

Directions:

1. Cook lentils by boiling in 2 qt. salted water for 25 minutes or till tender. Drain. Heat oil in a large nonstick skillet over medium-high heat. Add onion and cook for 5 to 7 minutes, until onion is translucent.

2. Place one-fourth cup lentils into a food processor; add 1 tbsp. flaxseed and 1 tbsp. water. Blend until smooth. Add flaxseed lentil mixture to skillet and cook for 1 minute. Add garlic, salt, and pepper; cook for 2 minutes. Mash mixture with a potato masher.

3. Combine the rest of ingredients in a food processor. Puree until the mixture forms a dough. Add one-fourth cup breadcrumb-walnut mixture to the remaining lentils in the skillet and cook for 1 to 2 minutes, until the mixture is dr.

4. Heat the smoker to 400° F. Line a baking sheet with parchment paper

5. Shape the lentil mixture into four 3-inch patties. Place patties on prepared baking sheet and bake for 45 minutes, until golden brown.

6. Put burgers on a bun with your favorite toppings.

Nutrition:

Calories 324;

Carbohydrates: 28.9g;

Protein: 13.6g;

434. SATISFYING VEGGIE ASSEROLE

| Preparation time: 15 minutes | Cooking time 50 minutes | Servings: 10 |

Ingredients

5 tbsp. olive oil, divided

6 C. onions, sliced thinly

1 tbsp. fresh thyme, chopped and divided

Salt and freshly ground black pepper, to taste

1 tbsp. unsalted butter

1 and one-fourth lb. Yukon gold potatoes, peeled and 1/8-inch thick slices

One-half. heavy cream

2 and one-fourth lb. tomatoes, cut into one-fourth-inch thick slices

One-fourth cup black olives, pitted and sliced

Directions:

1. Heat 3 tablespoons of the olive oil over a medium-high flame. Cook onions, stirring occasionally until they turn translucent. Sprinkle thyme and add salt and pepper to taste. Continue cooking for 5 to 10 minutes over a medium heat. Stir occasionally.

2. Heat a grill to medium-high. Brush potatoes with the remaining olive oil and arrange in a single layer on the grill. Cook for 8 to 10 minutes, until lightly browned, turning once. Cut into half- inch thick slices.

3. Preheat oven to 375ºF. Sprinkle olives on top. Pour the heavy cream over tomatoes. Cover and bake in the oven for 30 minutes or until bubbly and golden brown.

4. Enjoy!

Nutrition:

Calories 158;

Carbohydrates: 14.8g;

Protein: 2.3g;

435. NORTH AMERICAN POT PIE

Preparation time: 15 minutes	Cooking time 50 minutes	Servings: 10

Ingredients

2 tbsp. cornstarch

2 tbsp. water

3 C. chicken broth

1 C. milk

3 tbsp. butter

1 tbsp. fresh rosemary, chopped

1 tbsp. fresh thyme, chopped

Salt and freshly ground black pepper, to taste

2 and three-fourth C. frozen chopped broccoli, thawed

3 C. frozen peas, thawed

3 C. chopped frozen carrots, thawed

1 frozen puff pastry sheet

Directions:

1. Heat the oven to 450, and lightly grease a mug or small baking dish.

2. In a large bowl, dissolve the cornstarch with the water. Stir in the broth, milk, butter, rosemary, thyme, salt and pepper.

3. Add the vegetables and stir. Add the filling to the cooking dish.

4. Lay the puff pastry over the filling, and tuck the sides into the dish so that the pastry overlaps.

5. Bake for 50 minutes, or until the pastry is brown. Serve hot.

Nutrition:

Calories 257;
Carbohydrates: 26.1g;
Protein: 7.6g

436. POTLUCK FAVORITE BAKED BEANS

Preparation time: 15 minutes	Cooking time 2-3 hours	Servings: 10

Ingredients

1 tbsp. butter

One-half of red bell pepper

One-half of medium onion, chopped

2 jalapeño peppers, chopped

2 (28-oz.) cans baked beans, rinsed and drained

8 oz. pineapple chunks, drained

1 C. BBQ sauce

1 C. brown sugar

1 tbsp. ground mustard

Directions:

1. Prepare your Smoker and heat it for 450F.

2. Melt butter over medium heat and sauté the spices for about 4-5 mins.

3. Transfer the pepper mixture into a bowl.

4. Add remaining ingredients and stir to combine.

5. Transfer the mixture into a Dutch oven.

6. Place the Dutch oven onto the grill and cook for about 2-3 hours.

7. Serve hot.

Nutrition:

Calories 364;
Carbohydrates: 61.4g;
Protein: 9.4g

437. TRADITIONAL ENGLISH MAC N' CHEESE

  Preparation time: 15 minutes

 Cooking time 30 minutes

Servings: 10

Ingredients

2 lb. elbow macaroni

Three-fourth C. butter

One-half C. flour

1 tsp. dry mustard

1 and one-half C. milk

2 lb. Velveeta cheese,

Salt

black pepper

1and one-half C. cheddar cheese, shredded

2 C. plain dry breadcrumbs

Paprika

Directions:

1. Cook macaroni for 8-10 minutes under directed time in boiling water. Reserve 1/3 C. of macaroni water. In separate sauce pan, melt butter. Stir in flour and mustard until smooth.

2. Add milk and cook over medium heat, stirring constantly, until thickened and bubbly. Stir in cheese and macaroni water. Season with salt and pepper. Add cooked macaroni to saucepan and stir to coat with sauce. Garnish with the extra cheddar cheese and dust with the bread crumbs and paprika. Place in a smoky grill in a 300-degree Fahrenheit oven for 20 minutes or until golden brown. Serve immediately.

Nutrition:

Calories 914;
Carbohydrates: 99.9g;
Protein: 37.2g

438. AMAZING IRISH SODA BREAD

  Preparation time: 15 minutes

Cooking time 1 h + 15 minutes

 Servings: 10

Ingredients

4 C. flour

1 C. raisins

One-half C. sugar

1 tbsp. caraway seeds

2 tsp. baking powder

1 tsp. baking soda

Three-fourth tsp. salt

1 and one-fourth C. buttermilk

1 C. sour cream

2 eggs

Directions:

1. Preheat the Traeger grill to 375 degrees F. Mix the dry ingredients together in a large bowl. Be sure to measure and combine well.

2. Add the sour cream, eggs, and buttermilk into the dry ingredients. Mix until all of the ingredients are wet. Remove the dough from the bowl and form it into a rectangular loaf.

3. Bake for 60 minutes at 375 F. After 45 minutes, remove the baking sheet from the oven and spread what remaining dough there is into a wider loaf. Return to the oven for the last 15 minutes or so.

4. Allow to cool for 30 minutes. Serve.

Nutrition:

Calories: 340;
Carbohydrates: 63g;
Protein: 8.6g

439. NATIVE SOUTHERN CORNBREAD

Preparation time: 15 minutes	Cooking time 30 minutes	Servings: 8

Ingredients

2 tbsp. butter

1 and one-half C. all-purpose flour

1 and one-half C. yellow cornmeal

2 tbsp. sugar

3 tsp. baking powder

Three-fourth tsp. baking soda

Three-fourth tsp. salt

1 C. whole milk

1 C. buttermilk

3 large eggs

3 tbsp. butter, melted

Directions:

1. Sift together the dry ingredients. Then add the wet ingredients. Stir just until moistened, but do not overbeat.

2. Put a 3-quart cast iron skillet in the preheated oven and heat oven to 375 degrees. Pour the batter into the hot skillet and return the skillet to the oven. Bake cornbread for 25 to 30 min. until the top is golden brown. Remove cornbread from the oven and let it sit for 10 min. before serving.

Nutrition:

Calories 302;
Carbohydrates: 42.4g;
Protein: 8.7g

440. DECADENT CHOCO-LATE CHEESECAKE

Preparation time: 20 minu-tes	Cooking time 1 hour	Servings: 8

Ingredients

1 C. chocolate wafer crumbs

2 tbsp. butter, melted

4 oz. unsweetened baking chocolate, chopped

16 oz. cream cheese, softened

Three-fourth C. white sugar

2 eggs

1 tsp. vanilla extract

One-fourth C. heavy cream

2 oz. unsweetened baking chocolate, chopped finely

One-fourth C. white sugar

1 tbsp. unsalted butter

Directions:

1. Preheat the grill to 350 degrees F (175 degrees C). Grease a 9-inch springform pan. Sprinkle the chocolate cookie crumbs on the bottom of the pan.

2. Melt the 2oz. of unsweetened baking chocolate and 4 tbsp. of butter till smooth. Stir till.

3. Mix the cream cheese, 1/2 C. of sugar and the 1 tsp. of vanilla. Add eggs and beat till smooth.

4. Add the melted chocolate mixture into the cream cheese mixture. Beat till.

5. Pour the batter into a greased springform pan. Bake for 1 hour. Cool.

6. For the filling: In another bowl, beat the cream cheese, 2 oz. of unsweetened chocolate, 1/4 C. of sugar and 1 tbsp. of butter.

7. Beat until smooth. Add the whipped cream and beat till.

8. Pour the filling onto the cooled crust and refrigerate the cake.

Nutrition:

Calories 489;
Carbohydrates: 43.2g;
Protein: 9.4g

CONCLUSION

After building the smoker from a Wood Pellet Smoker and Grill Cookbook, you have had time to play and master your new smoker grill. You know how exactly to season the grill and the smoker. You have had time to learn the recipes and techniques for cooking on a smoker grill. You have completed your smoker grill cookbook. You love to try the great new recipes you have collected. You love your smoker grill more than any other piece of equipment in your great kitchen. You love all the great flavors you can achieve with your smoker grill. You love to eat, and you love to cook, and you love to improve the quality of your food with your smoker grill.

You have obtained every secret to cooking with a Wood Pellet Smoker and Grill Cookbook, and you have tons of great recipes to try again and again.

You have smoked and grilled many things on your exclusive Wood Pellet Smoker and Grill Cookbook. You have had many fine meals on your amazing smoker grill. You have experimented with many flavors in your awesome smoker grill. You have had more amazing, unforgettable, and rare dishes on your amazing smoker grill than you could ever process or remember. Every time, you can achieve the absolute best taste for your favorite food with your smoker grill.

You have learned to cook with your quality smoker grill, and you have given your family many wonderful gifts , Labor Day Weekend at your house. You have cooked for your family with BBQ Ribs. It was a great Labor Day Weekend. You had great ribs on your smoker grill. You had the best barbecue ribs that you have ever had in your entire life. You have had many occasions to cook BBQ Ribs in the delicious flavors you have achieved on your quality smoker grill. You love your smoker grill, and that is why you have made the best BBQ ribs on it every time you cook there for your family. You have made enough BBQ ribs in your life to have stopped the world and made those ribs a record..

Every day, your experience with the Wood Pellet Smoker and Grill Cookbook gives you the opportunity to get better at smoking and grilling. You can have the most amazing tasting food in your memory, every time you put it on your smoker grill. There are many ways to achieve great tasting meat. There are many ways to achieve great tasting vegetables from your smoker grill. You can get awesome tasting fish, poultry, and game from your smoker grill. You find all these tasty flavors in your food every time you cook.

You have become a cooking genius with your quality smoker grill. You can use your amazing smoker grill to get all of the delicious flavors in the wonderful smoked food you like so much. You can get all the best tasting food recipes and cook methods for a quality smoker grill. You love finding new in your smoker grill. You can achieve the greatest, most quality dishes with your amazing smoker grill. You are an incredible person for having built and mastering your awesome smoker grill. You can have the most amazing food flavors when you use your smoker grill.

CPSIA information can be obtained
at www.ICGtesting.com
Printed in the USA
BVHW010342080521
606756BV00008B/2022